Baby Naming Day

John Awen

Green Magic

Green Magic
5 Stathe Cottages
Stathe
Somerset
TA7 0JL
England
www.greenmagicpublishing.com

Typeset by K.DESIGN
Winscombe, Somerset

ISBN 9780995547803

GREEN MAGIC

Introduction

And so another journey begins. For me personally, writing this book has been an incredible journey, one of wonderment, seeking answers to questions that I didn't know I was asking until the answers appeared in front of me with the written word fluidly flowing from my four fingers, as that is the total amount of my typing skills. Any creative journey begins with what is in effect, a totally blank canvas. Any artist and I class myself in that genre as well as an author. Any form of creation is artwork; therefore, the creator is an artist, in one of many guises, whether that is with a chisel, a paintbrush, a keyboard, etc. To have an idea materialise randomly within your mind is an incredible gift, to be able to actually allow those ideas to manifest, in whichever form they may take is even more incredible. To be working on an idea, with no real direction to go forward, yet receive encouragement and support from those around you, loved ones, family, friends and in my case, a brilliant Publisher, who supports and believes in me totally, to the point of putting his money, where my words are, is a real compliment and a great accolade indeed, as anyone will appreciate. We all have ideas, goals, aspirations and dreams, many of which never leave the mind, whereas others, begin an incredible journey, as this book, along with my previous two books have. From an abstract and seemingly surreal idea, then onto a notebook, before forming in a word document within my laptop. After alterations, additions, corrections, along with editing, typesetting and other writing checks, it then comes into fruition within the pages of a book, which you are now reading, all in all, an amazing journey and one that I am so proud to be able to do. Like a new born child emerging from the womb, we watch them slowly grow, as with my book growing and taking shape. As with any parent, an immensely proud moment comes when you watch your child stand up and tentatively take their first steps, as I do once my book is released worldwide and for the public to see. You hope your child is going to stand strong on their own two feet and not fall down, it is no different for me watching the birth and growth of any book I write, you want them to stand alone and strong within the world.

Thank you to all those friends who have supported me along another magical journey. A big Thank you to Pete, my publisher, without whom, this book would not be. Thank you to those who have read various snippets of my early words and let me use them as a sounding board, to check that I wasn't totally going mad, or losing the plot more than anything. You know who you all are and I tip my proverbial hat to each and every one of you, Thank you.

I would like to say a massive thank you to Debi Wolf Reeves and her husband Andrew. Debi openly shared with me their heart breaking story of miscarriage, which is contained within this book. Throughout the long phone conversation with Debi, along with writing it, I shed several tears as Debi conveyed so eloquently their tragic journey of what was truly a life changing time for all involved. No parent should ever outlive their children it just goes against the grain and seems so wrong. To know that you are pregnant with child and then miscarry, for whatever reason, is just tragic and I cannot imagine and nor would I want to imagine, or comprehend the utter and total pain felt, by both parties. Thank you so much Debi and Andrew for letting me in and for so candidly sharing your story. Much love to you both and to Seren.

Baby Naming Day

The arrival or birth of any newborn into this world is nothing short of miraculous, in every sense of the word. To be up close and personal with the pregnancy and watch it come to full fruition with the arrival of a new child, is truly heart warming and an honour to be a part of. To slowly, over the months watch the swelling of a woman as she goes through what is the greatest event within the world strikes deeply within anybody the sheer complexities and total sacredness of the womb and from one seed, to see what happens and manifests from that is absolutely incredible and totally mind blowing. Beyond our comprehension and even though we know what happens, we still cannot fully understand how it happens. We are just spectators and mesmerised voyeurs in what is a magical journey of conception, growth and then arrival into this beautiful world.

As we look on, we see the foetus forming within the womb of the Mother, taking shape and manifesting into an innocent, pure and totally unadulterated newborn infant. The whole world feels and senses each new birth that comes into being. We feel every breath they take; we watch and encourage them to absorb life, to grow, evolve, to stand, to walk and to venture out into the world.

The unseen ethereal vibrations are felt throughout the universe and all of creation as we all become part of each child's journey, from the womb, into the world, from childhood right through to adulthood. We are all woven so tightly together that often we take it all for granted and can at times, become nonchalant and almost oblivious to it all.

If we tune in to what truly matters, centre ourselves and feel the life force within our own being, we can then feel the universal life force which beats and runs within each and every one of us and the world, along with all of creation as a whole.

We are all the same; we are just walking a different path to everybody else, as we all are. We need to now, as a collective, come together, put aside any differences we may have, or seem to have and strive to work and achieve the very reason we are all here in the first place. We arrive here in the same way and when it is our time to venture into the next stage of our being, we all leave the same way and go to the same place.

Life is too short and none of us know what is going to happen from one second to the next, let alone from day to day. We must all learn to not take a single second of the precious time we each have for granted, nor must we take anybody, nor anything for granted. Life is so very precious and this can be seen within the arrival and stirrings of each new child that arrives here to partake in their journey of life here on earth.

When the day to name our child does arrive, we give thanks, pay homage to the universe and set in motion an amazing series of events. Sheer, utter and total respect is given, shown and bestowed towards the whole universe, along with the new miracle of life which we have been blessed and gifted with. As we stand there to name a child, we are resonating with every being that has ever lived, is living and will ever live. We agree to endow this pure and innocent soul with a name, a label and the moniker that for all of eternity, they will be known by and be answerable to. An incredible time for all involved as worlds collide and the throb of the universe is felt and sensed by all within as a newborn is named on Baby Naming Day.

In this book, I am going to explore exactly what a name is, why we name, what some names mean, the importance and significance of a name. I will also explore the different ways we can celebrate a child's name, naming ceremonies, the most popular names and how they change with society's influences and fashions.

I am going to take myself on a journey, a fascinating one, which I hope, will ultimately take you, the reader on a journey also, giving my take and interpretation on all aspects of what is one of the most significant labels that we can have placed upon us by our parents, or guardians.

I sincerely hope you enjoy this book and if you would like to contact me, please feel free to e-mail me at spiritoftheawen@yahoo.com

Why We Name

A name carries a great significance. Next to our physical facial appearance, it is the highest standing and most appropriate way of identification for us. We take on the full meaning and relevance of the names which we carry, they remain with us throughout our whole lives, so it is imperative that we are gifted and blessed with one that is fitting and comfortable to wear. Unless at a later date we decide to adopt, or legally change our name, we carry it with us until we pass away. Even then, we will be logged, registered and remembered by our name, so it is vital that we personally like and connect with and to it.

We name our babies as without a name, we would probably still be nodding, grunting and therefore would still be performing a very primitive form of sign language, using nods, pointing and other gesticulations. Luckily, we have moved on and evolved significantly since those days and communication has rapidly changed, so now and for thousands of years, names have been placed and gifted upon us, normally at a very early age. A name presents us with a form of identification, a label if you like and as a way of recognition to others.

Having a name gives us a sense of belonging, an anchor and a feeling of being part of a tribe, or in a greater sense, as with some cultures, a part of the whole community. Names can be simple, easy and can also be extremely elaborate, it is entirely down to those who gift us with the name in the first place and what meaning is to be placed upon us.

Symbolism and intention are usually the mainstays for selection of a name, along with gender of the person who is to receive this honour, or distinction.

Basically, however we view a name, whatever meaning and symbolism we place upon it, a name is merely a glorified label and is the best, most widely used and primary way of recognition we have for one another. We can put all the magical intention we wish upon and into a name, but first and foremost it is a label, plain and simple and is the best way we have of physical identification.

A name can have much meaning and as well as gender, it can also show and reflect upon which country you, or your ancestors and parents originate from. A name can indicate something about the beliefs of parents and guardians. In olden days, people could see straight away from your designated title, or label, how much standing you had in a certain community, tribe, or village. More often than not, double barrelled names can show, even now, possible lineage connections and family strengths.

Names are infinite and many have been used for millennia. Some have disappeared in the mists of time, many have been eradicated, or obscured, whereas some stay popular, there are many that come back into fashion and establish themselves once again into our language.

There are many, many reasons why we designate, or opt for a particular name for our children, loved ones and also ourselves. Obviously, to those choosing a name, it is favoured and has been carefully chosen to be endowed upon the lucky and much loved recipient and above all, it is the intention of that name that matters beyond all else.

What is in a Name?

Names contain a multitude and plethora of various meanings; they can also be fairly simplistic. If we look back through the ages, names were basically designated to which tribe, or community you lived, worked and where part of. Our ancient ancestors would have had a fairly basic two, or three tiered naming system, which became accepted and easily recognisable to everyone within the village and wide spread communities.

The lower level of this system, peasant, basic

villager or serfs as they were known, had relatively basic names, denominating the type of work they did, Cooper, Tanner, Miller. The next or middle layer of this archaic system, often depicts which village they may have lived in, or can be seen to show that they were anything but lower level citizens. Names or titles could be such as, Peter of the Mill, Jack of the Pub, etc. The supposed top tier of this system normally reflected a standing within the community, which was a show of land ownership, high regards from others and monetarily influenced, like Lord, Lady and so on and so forth.

Since time began and Mankind slowly started to establish itself, there have always been those who seek power and control over others and as a show of self importance, what better and simpler way to achieve this, than decorating yourself with a name, badge, or label to proverbially show that you are better, or at least you think you are?

Often as a show of arrogance, people have labelled themselves with names simply because it makes them feel important, self righteous and can be portrayed as arrogant, egotistical in some cases and if we look back through history at some of the over the top and elongated titles, we can see this for ourselves.

So, what is in a name exactly? Well, as with anything, it is totally open to interpretation, various perceptions and a whole host of different understandings, all depending on how we see, view and sense it.

A lot of names which are used today and have been for centuries, can be labelled, or referred to as having Christianised connotations, names like John, Paul, Matthew and Mark are all related and seen as biblical, although I have no doubt at all they have been in existence since before that. Names like these and similar ones will always be fairly common as society does move with the times, to some extent, although these names are now firmly engrained upon our psyche and are still now, very popular and fitting.

As with anything, there are certain benchmarks we use to identify many subjects and items and this is no different with names. As mentioned we have certain monikers that are set in stone, easily recognisable and in constant usage, heard every day and we all know someone with one of these names, or have heard of them.

Within the multitude of names that we know and are easily recalled, some popular, some obscure, historic ones, elongated and shorter ones, there has been, over the last few decades a rise in what can be perceived as new, different, alternate names. I find this very warming and extremely endearing, as people are starting to realise that it is perfectly fine and socially acceptable to choose a name which is different and new.

Society is constantly changing and it needs to. We as humans need to accept changes that come along and happen as this is how we learn, grow and evolve. It's imperative and vital that we do not stagnate, but flourish, on all levels, allowing new growth and emergence of new beliefs, traits and benchmarks, some of which can obstruct and impede the constant flow of growth and strength around us.

This is why, the new energies and newly found names is so comforting and refreshing to see and hear. We have, or should be pulling away from the indoctrinated dogmatic structures of a world we have left behind. Years ago, nobody would have thought, or even contemplated naming their child Apple, Sky, Raven, etc, for fear of retribution and being ostracised by others, mocked and frowned upon.

As we now move and venture into a new and fairly unstructured way of life and living, we now realise that we can step out of the so called normality and seek newness, in whichever form, or forms that it presents and manifests itself to us. Revitalised abundant energies are now in full flow and this can be sensed in every aspect of life, so it makes total and perfect sense to start with the naming of a newborn child. From this point onwards, we are setting our hopes, dreams, aspirations and intent into the world. A child carries not only the hopes and dreams of his/her parents, but of society as a whole. There is no better place, or way to allow these to flow freely, than to bestow a new name and blessing upon the child, installing all that we can upon and in these pure and innocent souls.

A name, handle or label can evoke a vast array of meanings, disguises, hopes, fears, dreams and a plethora of other delights. It is these that we cast into the world with our intentions upon them and more often nowadays, these names are magically imbued and the full meanings and hopes behind them are only really known by the parents, or guardians that are choosing them and gifting them upon the child who will carry that blessing into the wider world, with pride, vigour and purity.

To have a child is an honour and a very rich blessing and to grant your child any name is also an honour and to have carefully pondered, thought and reached the point of deciding upon a name, is an incredible blessing also. To have asked for pointers, guidance and insights into his/her name is even more remarkable and very endearing. Take this journey of first finding out you are going to become a parent, with all the joy, careful planning and also chaos until the arrival, yet during that period of time, names, meanings and careful selection of a name are going round in your head as well. I seriously tip my proverbial hat to everyone who has made and been on this journey.

Reaching the decision of ultimately finding a name that totally resonates within both partners, if possible, is a light bulb moment. To arrive at a name, which you then know, beyond a shadow of a doubt, will sublimely suit and fit the newborn infant is nothing short of incredible and as you then proudly bestow that title upon them, you are setting forth and into motion everything you could possibly imagine and more, aspirations, delight, joy, love, hopes and pure unadulterated magical intent.

Let me ask the question again, what is in a name? Well, everything that you would like, or wish there to be can be held, captured and contained within a name, or you could cast out infinite intention upon it and then it also becomes an infinite and unlimited vessel of total magic. The choice is down to those who are embarking upon the journey, not only of careful choosing of a name, but a vast array of carefully planned selection of something a lot more special which will carry the child onwards into and through life. This is where the gift that is endowed upon the lucky recipient, the infant and their name, will hold them strong and shape who and what they ultimately become. Everything and so much more is held, yet also not held within a name.

Choosing a Name

Choosing a name can be instant, something strikes a chord deep within and it is there, straight away, on the other hand, we can at times, ponder long and hard, searching for that almost illusive special label, or name which is appropriate and fitting. Names can arrive in a variety of ways, a favourite place, a meaning, or a loved family member, at times, we hear a word that grabs us and that's it, the name is in place and we have arrived at it.

My loyal companion and best friend is my black

Labrador dog and he is called Pagan. I rescued him five years ago now, when he was two and a half, mind you, he chose me, so I believe he rescued me and we are united once again. His last owners gave him the name of Peighton, which I wasn't overly keen on, but didn't want to change it too radically, as I did not wish to confuse an already confused creature and soul. I had had him about a week, when I called him Pagan, he stopped straight away, ears pricked up instantly, so at that point, his new name was born and came into being. Very fitting really, seeing as we both love being outdoors and as I love nature and creation it was a very appropriate name to give him, he liked it instantly and so it came into being.

When we are making a discerned decision of choosing a name, as I have said, the name can, at times, be gifted and arrive to us instantly, which is great and within a split second, we can feel, sense and know whether it is the right one. Often we can search for an age, trawling through lists, place names, favourite books, lineage, and favourite films and so on. This can be an absolute overload on the senses and can often achieve nothing apart from creating tension and confusion.

As with many various aspects in life, we have to

wonder, do we choose a name, or does the name arrive and choose us, this is interesting and I am sure you will comprehend what I am saying there.

The society we live in and are a part of is less restrictive nowadays than it was, which is great as we can now feel freer to experiment and come up with a whole host and wider variety of names, however exotic, seemingly obscure and magical they may appear to others, we can do this, simply because it is now socially acceptable to try something new and different. We can still use and name our children, pets and ourselves with age old names as well, so it is up to us as individuals and couples, to appreciate this and arrive at any name that resonates within and also which reflects our beliefs, our ancestors, nature, anything we like. There is no structured table of names we have to conform to now, unless we wish to, the choice is infinite, simply because we can make up names as well, therefore it is limitless and in abundance.

Choosing a name, whether it is for our children, our pets, or even ourselves, if we wish to go down the road of changing our names, for whatever reason, leads us into a myriad of possibilities and questions. What would we like the name to symbolise and represent? Do we want to follow a tradition in any way and show that within the name? Is the name to show any particular reflection on our family, nature, our experiences, or do we just want a subtle name that is fitting for the gender of the infant? These are all possible questions and conundrums which may well present themselves once we begin undertaking the infinite plethora and varied assortment of names that are readily available, without assimilating one of our own making.

Gender used to feature strongly in the representation of a name up until recent times, that seems to have relaxed a lot as well, which in one way, is good, on the other side of the coin though, it can have its downfalls, as with anything, or any situation. On one hand, the title we are gifted with can be a huge blessing and we are more than comfortable to have it and be known by that chosen name. A famous wrestler had the name Shirley late last century, he was known by it, but not when he was fighting. I had a friend about twenty years ago called Tracy, which was fine, thing is he was Male and although he never changed it, I believe this could have started his anger off which stayed with him for many years, almost as if he was constantly on the defence, it makes you wonder. On the other side, there are people that choose and use names which are commonly known as being for the other gender, several rock stars and performers do this, maybe as a way of achieving instant recognition and getting noticed, who knows?

Way back in the mists of time, even nowadays within certain tribes, cultures and communities around the world, names were given, gifted and imbued to create a sense of power over the recipient, which could also strike fear into other tribes. A total show of power, strength and might that was known widely across the area that there would have been warring factions, ready to go to battle with each other over anything, land, politics and a host of other reasons. We only have to gaze upon some of the well known and historic names of chosen individuals to see that their very name could and would have struck fear into any possible enemies. Names such as Chief Sitting Bull, Boudicca Queen of the Iceni tribe, William Wallace, Attila the Hun, Eric Bloodaxe or Vlad the Impaler, these are to name but a few and these names alone would have had opposing troops nervous before they even got into battle.

There are characters and people throughout the aeons of history that deliver just what is intended within their name, fear basically, as if to thwart any opponents before any fighting takes place and many others have also become synonymous with death, cruelty and fear, so we can see now that if a mantle is fixed, many have and will rise up to live up to the powerful name that they have been given.

We can then look upon those who have names that are associated with peace and love, Mother Teresa, Buddha and the Dalai Lama to name but a few, these names only bring peace and serenity to others, so it just goes to show, fear, or the total opposite reaction can be reached and achieved, all within a name.

When we actually start to comprehend, realise and appreciate just how important a name is and what they truly say and reflect, we can see far beyond the basic labelling that names are so often seen as. They are a label, of course they are, every being and all of creation carries one, so that we can know and explain what and who we are talking about and making reference to, guidelines and benchmarks so to speak.

From birth, or just after we are gifted a name, we carry this with us throughout our lives and even when we cease to be and pass away, that name stays, etched and recorded in the eternal loop of history and time. Engraved in the echelons of the universe, our name and mantle remain visible for eternity and steadfast even if we choose to change our name, legally, or otherwise.

My surname at birth was not Awen, it was Higgleton. When I started writing properly around six years ago, in the year 2010, a lot of people started saying I had the Awen flowing through me. By this time I had already started to explore the earth based tradition, or belief, of Druidry. The symbolism of the Awen, is based entirely on the Celtic myth of Cerridwen and Taliesin. Taliesin became known as the first being who had the Awen (meaning shining brow) running through him. The more I wrote, the more this name resonated deep within me, along with all its various meanings, such as knowledge, wisdom and inspiration. In 2013, I made the decision to adopt this title as my surname and legally changed it. For me personally, I have taken on a very symbolic title, imbued and stoked with magic, mysticism, mythology and so much more. It also represents the constant ebb and flow of creation, life, abundance and inspiration, I absolutely love my new name and I believe it fits me well and assists me personally in all I do, strive for and am. Once again, I was gifted this name by many people who saw and recognised the burning fires of inspiration within me and I wear it with pride, honour and integrity, something we should all do. A gift from the universe, a name steeped in magic, which I gratefully accepted and adopted as my own.

Choosing a name is an incredible journey, however it arrives with you. From the millions of people who may have carried that name before, we can take it on and make it our own, we can let it evoke whatever we want it to within us and we can carry the baton of our label with pride. Names can be relatively short, or considerably long, that does not matter, what really matters is that whether we are selecting, or choosing a name for another, or ourselves, that we follow our hearts, signs we may get and that we reach a name that is right and endowed with love.

Gender within a Name

I touched albeit very briefly on this topic earlier; let's see what it really means now in more detail.

This is another very interesting subject and one that we can view and explore in two different ways. The names that are obviously designated for Males and Females specifically, and also the names that can easily be used and bestowed upon either sex, or genderless names if you like?

If we look at titles first and then go on from there, we can understand and take a better stance upon how this works, from very structured and allocated definitive sex titles and labels, then we can follow on from that to view more loosely based and less gender orientated names.

King, Emperor, Lord, Duke and Baron are all Male titles and there is no deviation upon these titles, they are set in stone and are totally designated for the Male, with absolutely no cross over area and interpretation. These labels have been part of our culture for hundreds of years now and we each know, when they are mentioned in the media, or in conversation that we are hearing, or talking about a Male role and title, no questions asked.

The Female counterparts, or equivalents to these titles are, Queen, Empress, Lady, Duchess and Baroness accordingly. Once again, there is absolutely no other way these titles can be seen, or given as they are strictly and absolutely for the feminine, or the Female gender, no recompose at all.

Within the Pagan tradition and many other beliefs and paths, there are the Masculine and Feminine beings, or divinities, the God and the Goddess, both of which are steadfast as to which gender they are and associated to and with. So when we look at titles, names and gender within this, we do have some definitive guidelines to associate and mark each sex with. It is a truly fascinating subject and highly complex, as with many different topics, there are interpretations that are so diversified and complex, that at times, we can become bogged down with it all and there seems to be no dilution to it. This is one of those infinite genres that we can become absorbed by, as it is a truly fascinating theme and within that, there are some stringent guidelines, which can be seen and which provide a point of reference for us.

If we now look at other names, which are usually connected with one, or the other gender, then we can see just how absorbing and infinite the choices are, once again though, it can come down to individual interpretations and personal choice.

Most names that we think of, just off the top of our head, have what we can perceive and are renowned as designated genders which they are more appropriate for than maybe the other gender. There are John, Mary, William, Catherine, Harold and Joanne, to name but a few. These names are well known and are Male and Female names respectively.

I am sure that any names you can think of and recall, probably have one sex that they can be placed upon in preference and are aligned more fitting than the other sex would be to place them upon? We then arrive at abbreviated names, which then take on a role and label all of their own and can readily and comfortably be placed upon both genders, Male and Female alike. Charles is known as a Male name, whereas the abbreviated version is Charlie, which fits and is used by and for both genders. Harold is a predominantly Male orientated name and Harriet is for the Female gender, shorten them both to Harry and this can be used for either sex, which is great and furthermore shows that it is all down to various understandings and interpretations. There are several names where this can easily be done and if we look closely, there are examples of this throughout history. A truly fascinating topic and one which, like many others becomes infinite once we start to look closely and basically deconstruct what appears to be steadfast and structured.

There are also a great number, which is growing rapidly all the time, of genderless or unisex names to choose from. These include names, which are as fitting and comfortable on Males and Females alike. Addison, Ash, Bobbie, Charlie, Chris, Dakota, Dale, Eddie, Elliott, Frances, Glenn, Harper, Jamie, Jordan, Kelly, Logan, Morgan, Pat, Ray, River, Rudy, Sam, Shawn,

Taylor, Val and Winter. All of these names, labels and monikers are and can be easily and readily be placed upon either sex, without appearing feminine, or masculine. Easily adorned by both genders and these names are appropriate for both, which shows once more how names can be given and bestowed without structure, yet each one of these names is a beautiful name for any child to carry through his or her life and can be done so very comfortably indeed and with great pride.

Popular Names

Whichever society or culture we live in, there are and have always been names which remain and prove extremely popular, regardless of age, or tradition. These names are embedded and etched firmly within the very blueprint of that culture and the people who belong to it. Traditions are spread widely across almost every aspect of our lives, wherever we live and whatever our personal take on various subjects is, some things remain and however much we resist these permanent benchmarks, they are also good to see and should be respected accordingly. Names are no different and some names have been around for centuries and remain with us to this day, some of these that have been around for many years are still in usage even now, which is great. No matter what period of time we find ourselves in, what happens and how much we try to resist, some things are better left alone and allowed to just stay with us, names are one of those topics. Emblazoned across the very essence and permanent basis of each society and intricately woven into and through the threads of all cultures, names are paramount and highly sought after, for obvious reasons.

There are many names that we can think of that have been in existence for countless years and many generations, in any walk of life and in many different societies, cultures and tribes throughout the world. Stalwarts and backbones of the countless and wide array of labels, or names that there have been and are to this day, forming a structure of solidity to what is an infinite and flexible subject. These particular names can be bestowed upon any individual and have been through the mists of time, from ordinary Men and Women, up to Kings, Queens, Lords and Ladies.

All names hold and carry a meaning; some of these meanings are, as with many different topics, steadfast, though they can also hold slight variations and interpretations depending on and according to language and culture. Many names are highly symbolic and very representational of a wide variety of topics and subjects, strength, love, deities, peace, places, lifestyles, flowers and countless other genres.

Countries and the society we live within are very often represented within a person's name, just as we would expect to happen. If the country or tribe you live in, and are a part of, have a Monarchy for instance, then often their chosen names are commonplace and have been in use for centuries by the people who inhabit that place. If we look towards religious orientated cultures and countries, then we can see that very often, the people choose biblical names for their children, as a mark of respect to the path, tradition, or religion that they adhere to and worship.

If we glance towards and at Pagan, or nature based communities and tribes, then we can easily and readily see that the names that are popular and more commonplace with the people there, reflect the lands, the elements and their chosen Gods/Goddess's and accompanying deities associated with their chosen and preferred path in life.

The countries in the Asian continent and the Far East often reflect names which have been carried by people for many centuries and are directly associated and linked to some of the oldest worshipped beings that we know of within today's society, such is their way of life and even though a lot of new names are emerging and being used now, many names are part of the backbone from times when their country was structured, based upon and built entirely upon their religion.

I find it absolutely fascinating that names can be so closely based upon and linked to just where they have derived and come from. We respect others, along with their chosen way of life, their history and all that comes with it. We also admire other cultures and find them very curious, the same can be said with names and although we honour other people's choices, they can seem out of place in another country. Imagine for instance, if a family of Native Americans moved into your town, city, or village, with names like Running Bear, Badger Mother and Young Doe. Would we be as respectful then, or would they appear alien to us, becoming a talking point of subtle mockery maybe?

Current fashions, as with anything, play a huge significance to what happens throughout the very diverse societies and cultures which we all live in and are a part of today and they have right through history. As we gaze back and reflect upon certain periods of time, we can see and highlight how and why certain names have been used so frequently and what it was that encouraged them to be so readily used at that particular moment in time.

If we ponder and look once again upon the regions and countries that we are born into, then we can see straight away that it is these places that play a huge significance upon our names and of those who are responsible for bestowing these names upon us at birth.

Our ancient and distant ancestors lived and worked the lands, they were foresters, craftsmen, builders and their names would have been representative of where they lived and also their chosen trade. Back then, obviously there was very limited transportation, except horses, or their own two feet for individuals to travel around on, so venturing out of the locality you lived and worked in, was almost unheard of, so a direct significance of this was shown upon the placement and locality of an area with the names they had and used. The village and hamlet they were born into and lived in was commonly used as a last name, or what we nowadays refer to as a surname. Others would carry their chosen profession, or the family business as a surname and this fashion would have continued and been in place for centuries. An easily understandable and recognisable way of expressing who you were, what you did for a living, also showing the family lineage and also incorporating the area in which you had been born into, lived and continued to labour and work in. Although nowadays to us, this seems fairly simplistic and without much thought, it was perfect, worked well and stood the test of time for many hundreds of years, therefore it was fashionable.

As the years moved on and times pass by, we can see different ways coming into being, one of these was the rigid and domineering structure of religious beliefs. The underlying and widespread connotations and hype that these carried was massive and are still in place to this day, though not as prominent maybe as they were many years ago.

Religion swept quickly across the lands and through all areas and communities, bringing with it enforced indoctrinations. From this resulting tidal wave of control upon the masses, a new fashion of names were included also, names which are still used today and in all walks of life. I am sure that we can all relate to these and probably know somebody called Matthew, Mark, John, or Paul? Several other names can be allocated to the religions which form a structured part of society nowadays and would have done even more so way back in time. Once again we can see and perceive how hype and fashion ultimately play a huge part on all aspects of life, the names, or labels we use so readily are not exempt in these and are a prominent part in them, they are no different and feature highly in the ever changing world and fashions especially.

We can look back upon the many aspects and fashions that come around into our lives and society as a whole and see that most of them are circular, they come in, drop out and most of the time, except for the more obscure and relatively unknown ones, they come around again, therefore going full circle, like a constant aspect. There are several names and monikers, as I have previously mentioned, that form the proverbial backbone of society, wherever that may be across the world and in all cultures. Names which are sewn into the very thread and existence of life, forming part of the very structure of humanity, therefore delivering us names we can count on and easily recognise, refer to and use freely, should we so wish to.

Nowadays, with all the advanced media, news stories and easy access which we have to the world around us, names can be heard so much more easily and readily than ever before, as with all genres and takes on life. We have film stars, pop stars and a numberless selection of beautiful, popular, strange and obscure names to choose from just here, names that become fashionable from these people and their children and become commonplace within the world. There is also a wider coverage of the whole world in general, more so than ever before. We have the internet, which brings us instant and total coverage, along with the explanations of any subject, or topic we choose to type in and take an interest with. Names are no different and we now have a much more varied and basically infinite choice of names in which to choose from and bestow upon our infants.

With all the new understandings that are now becoming established in all walks of life and across the globe, new and alternate names are coming into being regularly as well now, which is great to see and shows us furthermore that however structured a society is, or fashionable things are, any aspect of life is always open to and should readily welcome and embrace the new energies that come along and arrive. Names are no different here and as with anything, there is always room for more and different interpretations, whatever the subject, or nature of the genre is.

Lineage and Genealogy

Lineage and genealogy are both fascinating topics and more or less, they mean the same thing. How we have descended from our ancestors to where we are today and at this point in time. Our pedigree, the blood line we have stemmed from, our parentage and what has bought us to this point, basically how we have arrived at the now.

If we try and break it all down and ascertain how we have reached this point in time, we can then interpret it accordingly and as we see fit, along with how we perceive it, also, we can take the pieces which we are comfortable with and that which resonates within us.

We all have two parents, both of which, if we are lucky enough, are there throughout our younger and formative years. Unfortunately, as with many people, this is not always the case and a lot of people are devoid of one parent, or very sadly both, nowadays, we can normally find out from records offices, physically, or online, our birth certificates, or other records indicating our birth, which will then reveal our parents and our lineage, or blood line.

However easy, or difficult this task may be, it is truly fascinating and proves highly interesting, simply because it brings those we have never known to life, every single one of our ancestors is an intrinsical and vital part of us, our whole make up, our DNA and very structure. Without any of them, we would and could not be here now.

Once we look back at our parentage, along with our lineage and genealogy we are entering into an incredible journey, basically of self discovery, revealing names, places, professions and connections directly with those who have put us on the map of today and have undertaken a part in just who we are and will ultimately become.

Ancestors long gone and passed away hundreds of years ago, are suddenly remembered and bought back into being, as we slowly start to reveal where they came from, the jobs they undertook, who they married and what their names were. It is this magical symbolism of our names that is essential and as we reflect and draw on our past, the mists and shrouds of time slowly lift and dispel, revealing just how we got here, who was responsible for it and how infinitely long the lists of our lineage really are.

My own original name is of Irish Celtic descent and I have looked back through parts of my own lineage and history. On my Dad's side, I have revealed Police forensic photographers, a governor of Chelmsford prison in Essex and a well known Baptist minister, who, in his time, preached to the largest crowd known at Crystal Palace and also has a church named after him in Colchester, Essex, where I was born. More recently, my Granddad fought in the first battle of the Somme in 1916, he was wounded in this and I still have the shrapnel removed from his leg several years later.

If we do choose to follow our lineage and take up genealogy, what we find out and however far back we go, it truly brings the past and the people involved to life, albeit briefly. Basically, doing these searches, we are honouring those who have direct links to bringing us here to this point in time and we are then finding out who they were, how they lived, the children they had, it's an infinite and very incredible journey to venture into.

Our names are scorched and emblazoned upon and across the very fabric and map of time and history and it is us now, who have been gifted the baton of these almost timeless names to carry and run with, or adapt and change as we see fit.

Many centuries ago, the names we carry, or have carried were forged into the very blueprint of time and it is a culmination of countless beings coming together just at the right time in history, that have created, shaped and moulded everything that has been, is now and will be. The very significance of our names should not be underestimated, on one hand, they are simply a label which we carry and signifies to others, just who we are and where we may have come from. On the other hand, our names hold a plethora and multitude of beings, our ancestors, the paths they followed, the jobs they did, where they lived, who they knew and met and a whole host of other secrets, most of which are still waiting to be unlocked and discovered. Some of these secrets may never be unlocked and neither will they be revealed. The very essence of the universe holds everything in its infinite memory and databank, so there we, along with our names are held constantly and will be for all of time.

To discover just who we are and have been connected and related to is a very humbling journey, not only of self discovery, but a discovery of those recently and long passed away, the very ancestors which have helped make us who and what we are now.

The very origins of our names, labels and monikers may seem basic, but look again, you will see it differently and not only can we bring our very name and essence to life, but also those who have forged and put their own personal stamp upon our names, which we carry with pride today. If we are lucky enough to become parents, then these names will carry on another generation at least, effectively passing the mantle onto our children and infants which we gift and endow our name upon.

Baby's Arrival into the World

From the very first moment of sexual intercourse and conception, where a baby is created deep within the Mother's womb, the sperm from the Male penetrating the egg in the ovary, leading from and to all of these actions and associations, which truly are an incredible and nothing short of miraculous sequence of events, something we so often take for granted, because we struggle to comprehend it. All of these interactions form an amazing chain of events, from this a very precious transformation and journey begins, not only for the newly bought into being foetus, unborn and unformed infant, but both parents. I understand that throughout the world and history, there are not always two people present during the term of pregnancy, but for this book and this section, we will assume that there are both parents present right throughout the nine month term of pregnancy.

For anybody fortunate enough to find themselves with a pregnancy, which is a very rich blessing and gift indeed, probably the most precious gift there is, life slowly changes, on all levels, physically, mentally and spiritually. To be able to feel new life slowly coming into fruition must be an incredible, if somewhat daunting at times, adventure. For the Female, who obviously is the sacred and divine bringer of life, the onus is endowed upon her, more so than her Male counterpart, who proverbially and physically really, is only needed once, to seed the egg inside her.

Once a pregnancy is formed, deep within the sacred space of the womb, an unrivalled series and sequence of events take place, unlike any other. This is of course, happening to and for both the parties involved, the unborn and slowly forming infant and also the Mother who is carrying this new growth of life deep within her body.

On all levels, across the spectrum, physically and metaphysically, both bodies are changing, one forming totally from a seed and an egg, the other body is now undergoing the biggest transition and transformation possible. Two bodies, growing, one forming and the other supplying the essential lifeline of growth and vortex of space and energy needed, which is imperative for growth and sustenance for the as yet, unborn infant. A multitude of changes happens daily and these incredible changes are often so minute and unseen, that they could almost go unnoticed and unfelt. It's only when you actually look at the details of these events and strip them back and down to basics, that these small changes are actually relatively large, especially when you look at and analyse the whole and bigger picture. An amazing metamorphosis is happening constantly, a journey so inconceivably complex and mind boggling, that even though we know how and what happens, it is still fundamentally one of the hardest for our minds to understand and fully comprehend. Life cannot be replicated, not on this level and even if we could, the beings which may result would and could not be the same as the sacred life created and forged from the divine Male and Female, whichever species we are talking about.

There are many symptoms and side effects caused and associated with pregnancy, now obviously these are not the same for every Mother to be. Some of the most common are morning sickness, which can last weeks, or can sometimes last the full term of pregnancy. Swollen joints are common as well, due to the extra weight that is being carried during this time. Obviously, the stomach swells, depending on how large the baby is, how small the Mother to be is and water retention plays a massive part in this as well. Backache is another commonly felt pain, or ache at this time. Carrying the extra weight once again, which effectively pushes a woman's pelvis out of line to compensate for the growth and formation of the infant she is carrying inside her. Another frequently felt side affect at this time is Indigestion and heartburn, not nice at all and this is believed to be caused and more than likely is caused from the very fact that the Mother to be's stomach is being constricted hugely, pushed upwards causing the stomach acids to rise accordingly. There are a host and a multitude of other symptoms, but they can come and go and are totally different for each pregnancy and each Female will experience pregnancy in an alternate way to another, no two are ever the same.

As well as feeling extremely tired and lethargic physically, this tiredness can encroach on the mental state and health at the same time. Even though there is new life forming, which is a natural time of high energies and abundance, a Female Mother to be can often be left feeling totally drained and depleted, as if they are having the life literally sucked out of them, which in effect, is exactly what is happening, as one body vessel and supply is now working to sustain and maintain the health of two beings, working in harmony and balance, also at full and extended capacity.

There are many jokes and anecdotes about how tough a pregnancy is, not just for the future Mum, but also the Father. How long suffering they are and how they put up with their Female counterparts nagging, moaning and constant demands for obscure food stuffs and a host of other wants, needs and demands. This is par for the course and is probably over played extensively; it is just now set in stone and is part of any pregnancy now.

When we look at this absolutely incredible journey that both parties, male and female are now on together, it is amazing that as well as going through this together, not even mentioning the night sweats, sleepless nights and sheer discomfort the woman feels, often throughout the whole term of pregnancy, that a name for the unborn infant is often thought about, toyed with and at times chosen before the birth. Nowadays, the sex or gender of the unborn child is known and the parents can be made aware of it, should they decide to be told, at around three months into the pregnancy.

To think that even with all the normal and everyday tasks to do and compete with, work, cleaning, shopping, bills, etc, two people are now going through a very magical, on one level massive change in who they are and their lifestyle with the knowledge that they are both going to be parents very soon. On the other side of the spectrum, the worry, stress and facing the unknown, which being blessed with a birth is? With all of this going on for and around them both, it is inconceivable really that this is the time when a name is being chosen to be gifted and endowed upon the yet unborn infant, incredible really.

The arrival or birth of a baby is and can be extremely emotional and very traumatic, for all parties involved. The Mother is going to be in a state of utter and total sensitivity, feeling unsure, frightened, relief, immense pain and total elation and exhaustion, both during and after delivery of her newborn baby. Feelings and tensions will be felt like never before, a much heightened state physically and emotionally. Giving birth to new life must be the most endearing and humbling experience to have, I have witnessed it myself once with my own Daughter and many times when I have watched animals give birth and it is truly humbling and an absolute honour to witness first hand. Let's say the father is privileged enough to be at the birth of his child as I was. To watch your partner going through this is a very tense and incredible journey. I felt totally useless and inadequate as I watched the mother of my child screaming, sweating profusely and writhing in agony on the bed in the hospital. It was very surreal looking back, as I watched in bewilderment at all the Doctors, Nurses and a Midwife trying to make her as comfortable as possible during a very intense time. Then, seemingly out of almost nowhere and amongst all the chaos, I was thrust this newborn baby, looking quite off colour and spattered in blood, a very unreal, but very real moment indeed.

Let us now turn our attentions and focus to this pure and innocent new life that has just been through probably the biggest trauma there is that anybody can go through. When you think of it like that, it makes us see and view things very differently indeed. Suddenly thrust into a world where you're every sense is on overload. Loud noises, bright lights, smells and a whole host of other sensory delights to contend with. A far cry from simply floating in the amniotic sac that has held you safely for nine months and sustained your growth and development. Welcome to the world little child.

I find it very cathartic that during one of the most emotional and stressful times in people's lives, they manage to receive and reach moments of clarity and insights as to find a name for their off spring. There are occasions where, upon the arrival, or birth of the baby, the chosen name, for whatever reason does not seem fitting after all, maybe it doesn't resonate quite right, in which case another name is chosen and gifted accordingly. These moments are fairly uncommon, by all accounts, but it does invariably happen at times as it is bound to.

A huge time of celebration now ensues as another innocent and pure soul is birthed into the world and universe. The new parents certainly have a lot of changes to make and total alterations are now being felt and put into place on the new family unit as a whole. Where there was just two people, (if this is a first child), who are both relatively self sufficient and capable of surviving on their own merits and instincts, that all changes now with the arrival and addition of a new member to the family. A totally helpless individual who is reliant on his/her parents for everything. Where a routine was in place that suited both parents, that now disappears and the proverbial zone of comfort which was enjoyed before, is now suddenly and literally eradicated and is gone forever more, to be replaced with a family unit that are now to grow and evolve together as one. Sleepless nights, endless nappy changing and constant feeds now replace cosy nights curled up on the sofa watching films that both parents blissfully enjoyed together as a couple before the infants arrival.

The emergence of new life is a great joy, not just for the parents, but for all the extended family, along with neighbours and people who see you holding, carrying, or pushing a new baby about. Everybody knows, feels and senses the sanctity of new life, even if they are unaware that they do. The most precious of gifts and sights to see, beyond all comparison is the ultimate blessing of pure, unadulterated innocence and perfection that is a new arrival into the world, of a newborn baby and infant.

After a few weeks, or months, depending on the situation for each family, a naming ceremony is often thought about. Obviously, depending where in the world you live, the legal registration of a birth comes first, normally this is done within a few days, or a couple of weeks of the child's arrival and this is totally different to any naming ceremony which ensues.

Naming of Infants who do not Make It

I am sure we all know of someone, a family member, close friend, or maybe people reading this book have suffered the absolute trauma and terrible circumstances of having a miscarriage, or a still born birth? To even contemplate this and attempt to imagine the horrific devastation that such a tragedy can bring, is heartbreaking and I cannot and do not want to imagine the intense and sorrowful feelings that would be associated with either of these situations.

I could not leave this section out and for me personally, this book would have been unfinished and incomplete if I did not include a section on what is one of the most awful situations that any parents can possibly find themselves in. I am not even going to try and comprehend the heightened and intensely fraught emotions that are associated with such a tragedy. What we need to remember is that these precious and sacred souls, who, for whatever reason did not survive to make it into this world and if they did, it was just for a fleeting visit, need to be remembered, cherished and named.

A very dear friend of mine, Debi Wolf Reeves, kindly offered to share with me her and her husband's story of how they both longed to be parents, shared the joys and sheer elation together as they found out that Debi was pregnant, only to suffer the crashing blows of a miscarriage.

Debi kindly and very calmly spoke with me and divulged these intimate moments, along with the harrowing times, culminating in the knowledge that it was not their babies time on earth, yet they both know and totally understand their lost baby, is with and around them both and in all they do. These are not quotes, they are my words and taken from the story and truth that Debi tenderly shared with me. Debi, her husband and I, can only hope that in writing this section, however hard it is to read, that somebody, somewhere, may find peace, comfort and solace in the fact that they are not alone in their grief and suffering. My head is bowed in grief, and was from the very first moment Debi shared their story with me. I am honoured to have been confided in enough for them both to openly tell me this and to be able to pass it on to a wider audience through this book, thank you.

It is a very sad fact, that even with the modern technology and health care that the majority of us are blessed with and fortunate to have access to, that one in four pregnancies ends in a miscarriage, that's a quarter, an alarming and extremely sad statistic indeed. Most of the time this happens within the first three months of pregnancy and invariably miscarriages happen for a multitude and assortment of reasons. One of the reasons a miscarriage will happen and the most common one is that even though the egg has been successfully fertilized, it fails to start forming properly, possible through some deformity.

Once this starts to happen, the sacred body and female womb, recognizes this and starts to reject the egg, basically registering and seeing it as a harmful toxin and poison, which must be got rid of. This is incredible and also very sad to understand. The body will hold, nurture and feed a healthy pregnancy, yet as soon as an adversity, or malfunction is picked up within it, the body has to protect itself, resulting in the repelling of the threat, in this case, the faint throb and as yet, unformed infant within the sacred space of the womb.

Debi and her husband shared the intense elations, joy and sheer magic of realising that they were both going to become parents, what an utter joy for any couple to behold and a time of celebration for them both and also those closely linked and associated with them. Debi told me, that even though she felt and knew within herself that she was pregnant, she still kept doing the pregnancy tests; around twelve all in all, bless her. Debi even took a picture of one of the tests, showing the positive result, to keep for posterity and to remember it was really happening and was very real.

Between them both, they started imagining having a new life in theirs, names were being thought of, which colours to decorate the nursery in, the clothes to choose and a whole host of other maternal and paternal ideas and instincts were now starting to manifest between them both, a very magical and special time indeed for them both.

Debi was enduring a lot of the symptoms associated and experienced with a typical pregnancy, the morning sickness, aching joints, etc and as a yoga instructor and teacher, was very in tune with her body and was fully aware of safe moderate exercises, which are vital to keep the body in trim and to remain centred, grounded and balanced, important always, maybe even more so at times like these.

It was while doing some very gentle yoga moves, that Debi felt a twinge right inside her womb. Being extremely attuned and physically aware of her whole body and being, Debi knew and sensed immediately that her pregnancy was over, beyond any shadow of a doubt, at that instance, she knew she was losing her baby. This was in 2013 and Debi was 44 years old.

This happened on a Sunday, on the Monday, the day after, Debi got up in the morning and noticed there was blood in her urine, which can be fairly common during pregnancy, often referred to as spotting, this simply reiterated what Debi already knew, basically, she was losing her unborn child at around eight weeks into the pregnancy.

Calls were made to the hospital and an appointment was made to attend the hospital for the following day, Tuesday. Debi and her husband Andrew attended the appointment where an ultrasound was performed. Debi said it was a very hard, emotional and traumatic time for them both. They were now seeing, from the womb, the very spark, essence and heartbeat of their child, yet it was not going to be, they were losing their unborn infant.

Another appointment was made for the next day, Wednesday. Debi and Andrew duly kept it and a further ultrasound was performed. At no point was Debi told she was having a miscarriage, but was told that the positioning of the foetus was totally wrong. Being an intuitive and perceptive person, Debi was already aware that she was losing the baby on the previous Sunday and these appointments were basically just going through the procedures which were needed.

The next day was Thursday and Debi recalls it was a beautiful day, late summer, so Andrew and Debi took a leisurely stroll in the fresh air, which as you will all know, being outside is a great way to put life into perspective? Later on that day, while relaxing on the sofa, Debi suffered extreme and excruciating abdominal cramps. Having visited the loo, Debi was not surprised and also heartbroken, that there was a significant amount of blood being emitted.

Andrew phoned the ambulance and Debi was taken straight to their local hospital, placed in a private room and was monitored thoroughly constantly. After a couple of hours, another examination was undertaken and it was at this point, Debi, intentionally, or not, released and expelled the entire residue which was inside her womb. After being cleaned up and watched further for a while, Debi was told she could go home and just to be careful and gentle with herself. An appointment was made to see a Midwife, which is vital after a miscarriage just to make sure there is nothing remaining within the womb.

Even though Debi never experienced giving birth, she told me that having and enduring the miscarriage was the worst pain that she has ever gone through, physically, emotionally and spiritually.

Debi and her husband Andrew had already chosen the name for their Daughter and she was to be called ' Seren,' which means star. A while after this tragedy, they both had remembrance tattoos. The pentacle was inked into them both to symbolise their loss and the life gone of their departed daughter, Debi and Andrew had these sacred remembrance tattoos inked over their hearts and in doing this, they were asking the God and Goddess to hold Seren in their warm embrace until they could all be joined together and reunited in the Summerlands.

Several pieces were put in place as a way of connecting and remembering their lost daughter. A Pyrocanthus plant was purchased and planted in the garden and in their local woods, near Sherwood Forest, England, an old Beech tree was chosen as a shrine to Seren. This provides a haven away from their home to visit and remember their daughter, where ribbons, notes of love and other offerings can be placed. A sanctuary where Debi and Andrew can frequently visit and pay homage, show love, cry, smile and vocalise their innermost feelings to Seren until they all meet again.

Later on in 2013, Debi performed a naming ceremony in her back garden. She performed this on her own in front of an altar and had a candle burning. This provided peace, comfort and a total sense of connection to and with Seren. Her daughter who started to form within Debi's womb, they sensed one another, formed a bond and connection, yet it was not meant to be, so they never actually met and Debi, along with Andrew, never cradled and held this beautiful young, innocent and pure soul who was their daughter. Not only was this a very poignant time, it was a naming and passing over ceremony combined together.

Any loss of an infant is a terrible tragedy and millions of people, sadly, experience this. Whether through a miscarriage, a still born birth, or simply because an infant is not long for this world and has to return to the Summerlands, we should all take the time to remember them fondly. No parent should outlive their children, no matter what we believe, it goes against everything and all I know is that some lives are just not supposed to be.

I would like, once again, to take this opportunity to thank both Debi and Andrew for sharing this story with me and all of us hope that in sharing this story, we may give strength, peace and comfort to those who are unfortunate enough to suffer a situation like this. Much love to you all.

Naming Ceremonies

If we look across various different faiths, paths and religions, there are a myriad of different interpretations and takes on baby, or infant naming ceremonies. A whole host of ideas, ways and traditional views upon this important and very sacred event. Some of them may seem fairly obscure, almost alien to us, that doesn't matter, what is important is that all over the world, in various cultures, societies, communities and countries, children are being named, acknowledged and therefore, presented to the wider world as a named being that has been endowed with a moniker, a label and therefore is recognisable and identifiable from that name.

If we gaze back through the mists of time, revealing the way our ancient ancestors would have gone about naming their children and kin, we can see that the representation from then, right through to the present day, is really not that far removed and can be compared and recognised easily today as attributing the major parts and various, in effect, ceremonial similarities, right throughout time, heralding the same outcome, to gift, grant and bestow a sacred name upon an infant.

Back in days gone by and this would have been commonplace basically, in which ever society, culture, or community you lived in and were a part of, the newborn baby would have been held aloft for all to see and their name would have been shouted out, more than likely by the child's father, or elder of the tribe, who may well have delivered, or been present during the birth, in recognition and acknowledgement to the people there present.

After this holding aloft, which signified another new life and abundance for all the tribe, clan, or community, a huge time of celebration would have taken place and ensued. This momentous occasion could have and invariably was celebrated, honoured and worshipped for several days. The whole village and community would have freely and readily gathered together, bringing with them whatever foodstuffs and drinks they would have had available to them. Depending on the significance of the child born, other communities would have been invited as well to join in this very special time. Obviously, this would have been a major event, when you consider there was no contraception available then, there was more disease which could so easily kill and none of the modern healthcare we have access so readily to nowadays, a child being born was probably the highlight of any group of people and huge revelry would have followed the arrival of each individual born into that group.

Our ancestors would have held sacred their different Gods/Goddesses and all the deities they followed and worshipped. They would have held them in the highest esteem and looked to them and honoured them totally and whole heartedly in all they did and undertook. These deities would have been essential and great reverence was paid to them constantly, for the tribe, or communities crops to flourish, for the animals they kept and slaughtered for food and clothing, their homes and all the new life they were blessed with. Each crop that came to fruition meant that group would survive another winter and would be able to stock their larders and each newly born infant that was gifted to them, meant that their tribe would survive and so their lineage and group would carry on. The significance of each birth back then cannot be compared to our survival and existence nowadays, simply because the majority of us live in a cultureless society, where we have seemingly lost our way and our connections to the natural world have become disjointed and are almost nonexistent.

Each baby conceived and born is equally as essential and a huge blessing as much as every other one, it's just where we have become so lost as a race, we have become removed from the reality of our very survival and the significance of each one of us.

I am not detracting from any birth in the slightest; they are all a huge gift and blessing. If, lets say, our village, group, or clan depended imperatively on each new infant for its very survival, then we may be able to grasp what the huge significance of an infant being birthed into that group would have been and meant to everybody involved. Not only as a powerful sign from the Gods/Goddesses' they intricately followed and worshipped that their community was being blessed with new life, for them it would have meant and signified fertility on all levels, their homes, the people there as well as all their animals, the crops they planted and tended to, along with each member of their village, or tribe.

Abundance, good fortune, health and a remonstration that they were living a life of truth to their deities and all they undertook was needed constantly, for all their survival and for each person involved, a new child being born to their village was immeasurable and of great significance to every single member living, residing and working there. Beyond our comprehension nowadays, but if you truly think about it, with all the basics and inconceivable threats our ancestors lived with constantly, physically, mentally and spiritually, then it is not so hard to imagine. Beyond all else, the two things they relied on more than anything, was the safe harvesting of their crops, ensuring life would be retained through nourishment and sustenance. The second part of this is that their group would be physically fertile and gift new life and children into the tribe, this ensured the longevity and survival of them all for many years to come.

Since the earliest days, holding aloft a new born infant, has been an incredible and very significant occasion. With this fairly basic, yet instinctual symbolisation of beautiful new life, what is happening is a show of immense pride of new life venturing and being born into the wider world, also, at times without realising, it is paying homage and honouring the chosen deities, who have granted this child to the parents, or guardians who are blessed with the arrival of the newborn.

Often, the newborn would have been gifted their name minutes after the birth and arrival into the world. All the villagers, tribe, clan, or community members would have gathered to show and express their happiness and celebrations would have ensued, during which time, everyone would have said thanks to their Gods/Goddesses and savoured together this very special time. Quite often, an anointing of the child would have taken place as well. Anointing can be as basic, or as elaborate as you wish, it can be just a drop of water placed, or dripped onto the forehead, or it can be water splashed onto the face, or a complete immersion and submergence of the individual into a stream, or water vessel.

The significance and symbolisation of water is

fairly obvious really. It is a major life giving force within and without us. Every living being, human, animal, plant, tree, etc, relies upon it and without it, we would all fail, shrivel and fade away. Water is also a cleanser, a purifier, soothing, refreshing and a bringer of life. The importance of anointing cannot be denied and has been used as a representation of the divine beings and entities we follow and worship. As we are all divine beings anyway, it is extremely fitting and of great significance to who, and what, we are.

Parents and their Choice of Names

The names we are endowed with by our parents, or guardians, are special, meaningful and symbolise a myriad of various meanings and are of importance to them. While we are receiving and being gifted with these names and labels, they hold absolutely no significance to us whatsoever, partly because we are not aware of it and can't remember being named and by the time we do take it all into consideration and think about it, we are oblivious to them and just act, answer and respond accordingly and as we are expected to.

I think it is par for the course and totally normal for any young child who reaches a certain age, to question their name, almost like a rebellion, like refusing to eat the food in front of you, it's about the only other way you can attempt to make a stand at such a tender age.

I personally remember asking questions as to why I had been called John and I must have only been around six years old, then again, I questioned everything. I think it is all part of the adjusting, finding, becoming and accepting process, which can awaken at different and varying times within us all. From what I can remember, for me it was normal to question everything and I was often asking my parents if they could change my name and basically why they had named me that in the first place? Looking back and reflecting upon it now, it wasn't because I disliked my name, I just wanted to take a stance, make a stand and question it all. I asked why I wasn't called a more popular and fashionable name, when I was told it was all of those things, I turned it round and wanted to know why I hadn't been called a rarer name? My poor parents, I was challenging them constantly and at every turn, even from a very young age.

All of us know of some very obscure names which we are glad that we were not endowed with, names which I will not suggest or write here, as it wouldn't be fair and I know we all have aversions to certain monikers, some that seem so obscure and extremely strange, alien to us and almost embarrassing , then again, to the person who is wearing that label, it is of great significance and holds memories, meanings and is perfect for them and a worthy name to have, wear and be proud of. It is all down to our own take and interpretations upon it, how much we favour it, like it and who named us with it. As we reach an age where we can see and perceive all these undertakings and how we came to be known by and with that name, we can accept it more readily and easily, so we acknowledge it more and become proud of it.

Names arrive to the deliverer from a whole variety and a multitude of aspects, experiences, lineage, icons, or they can arrive out of nowhere and seem very fitting and resonate within them, so at that point, a new child's name is selected, approved by all involved, then gifted to the newborn infant. Totally ignorant, unaware and oblivious of this symbolism being granted upon them the child is merely heralded and paraded around with a new label and name granted upon them, which at that age, means absolutely nothing to them at all.

Once again, we can complain about it from an early age, as I did, but that's just game playing, without the realisation of the game, we are merely trying it on. Once we attune ourselves into our bodies, our skin and our whole being, then we start to perceive and sense the world around us, along with who we are very differently, it can be from this moment that we either truly connect and resonate with our name, or we might go the opposite way and shy away from it. If we decide, for whatever reason on the latter, that we really do not like the name we have been gifted with, then a painful and slow process can entail and ensue. That does not have to be the case, we can just technically morph into a new name, without any fuss at all, let's look at both parts and aspects of these decisions now, trying to ascertain what could happen, in both cases.

If we reach an age, or the understanding within us, that we really do not like the name we have been given, granted and had bestowed upon us, this can of course have many and varying ramifications and they can be restricting, burdening and make the wearer feel oppressed, weighted and heavily negated.

A name is so much more than any of us can ever really comprehend, it can be a stigma, a massive weight to carry and something that makes the bearer feel wretched and embarrassed by the sheer mention, or muttering of it. This is of course, an extreme, yet it does happen, its nobody's fault, it is just part of knowing, becoming and acknowledging the true self and how you would preferred to be seen and known as.

We can nullify a name, we can shrug it off, all the invariable name calling and connotations that may arrive, or derive from it. What if though, it makes the wearer so depressed and saddened by the sheer mention of it, feeling as if they want to recoil and retract away from it? There are ways of overcoming this and the easiest and most common, which avoids any legal name change and a very popular one, especially in years gone by, is to, if you have a middle name and it is any better, just change them around and become known by that name instead. I know and am aware of several people who have done this, some from a relatively early age and it works for them, really well and with this basic and easy change around of their names, they are lightened totally and have a new lease of life so to speak.

Our names embody just who and what we are, so to fulfil ourselves personally, on all levels, it's imperative to have and be known by a name that fully resonates within us and one that we are totally comfortable with wearing and appreciative of being known as. To excel and achieve, in all walks of life, along with all our levels of consciousness, we have to be totally at ease and comfortable, if we are not, even in the slightest way, then it can start to eat away at us, therefore negating who and what we are.

The names we have and are known by are vocalised many times a day and are written or printed across all of our identification documents and messages which we receive, so basically we can never escape it. We are that name and that name is us, so it is vital to our well being to love and connect with our names. If this seemingly small fact is not comfortable to and with us, it needs to be changed to allow us to become vibrant, whole and at peace within our very self.

Legal changes of name are fairly commonplace nowadays, they are relatively easy to do, cheap and most solicitors are able to facilitate and undertake them. For a small fee, you can walk in with your identification, which proves who you are, fill in some forms, sign in your old name, along with your newly chosen and designated title and name and that's it, done. You get a new name and a new lease of life, which for those who are really burdened by their name must be so rewarding and empowering. It really is and can be the seemingly smaller pieces of our lives, which can make the most important and significant changes to who we are and what we are.

On the plus side of having a name, many people and individuals embrace and totally connect with the names they have been given from birth, they accept them, never question them and are free and happy with the choice made for their names, by either their parents, or guardians.

As with anything, there is always a balance, there has to be and these two sides of the same coin, explain and show that perfectly. There are always extremes, in all we do and undertake, these total opposites of a scenario also show us just how detrimental the most simplest matters and insignificant to others, can have the most damaging, or enlightening of affects upon one another.

Appropriate, and Significant, Names within the World

Names, like other parts of the society we live in, such as the foods we eat and the languages we use can be attributed and ascertained to the cultures we live in, along with the tribes we have originated from. The main significance, trait and giveaway of where we hail and come from, is the language we use, or the accent, which can change from county to county and also vary quite a lot from suburb to suburb.

I find it absolutely fascinating, that if we ponder on names from around the world and the names within tribes, like the indigenous aboriginal people of Australia and other regions, the Inuit's of the arctic areas and the Native American Indians, we can see how nature based their names are? Taking their way of life and how they see and sense the world around them, which is pure, heartfelt and of substance, the strengths they have, show and use, often in the face of travesty and adversity, reflects their openness and purity to all beings and the wider world, which they work closely with, show utmost respect to and see as sacred. The names they have and still endow upon their newborn infants, shows us all that somewhere through the maelstrom of it all, we are missing the point totally.

Unadulterated, free from the indoctrinations of others, without prejudice, malice and not as weighted with structure as we are in our very Western civilization, packed with greed, we see everything and everyone as a commodity, there to extort and exploit constantly, more for financial gain than anything else, it's no wonder we live so very differently and this is shown in all we do and firstly, most noticeably, we can see and hear it in the names and labels with which these proud people use and gift their young ones with.

A reflection upon what is around us, how we are governed and controlled, has a direct input upon how we view the world, how we think, act and our take upon daily activities within our lives. All the cultures and peoples I have mentioned in this section, take and derive their names from the world around them, the weather, the animals, the elements and the wider, beautiful and natural world, which they work closely with, live off of, respect, acknowledge and know they are linked tightly to and with it.

A realisation, recognition and the very acceptance of the fact we are tightly woven into the very fabric of creation, deludes so many of us, we have become disassociated with the very world which holds, cradles, sustains and nurtures us. We now see that we are above the natural world, we seek our pleasures now in manmade creations, removing ourselves even further from what truly matters.

In the wider societies most of us inhabit and recognise, names linked and derived from animals, rivers, the weather and so on, are now, slowly starting to make and form an appreciated and designated place for themselves, which is great to see and shows us all, that there is hope and so long as we can interpret life in general, then there is a place for alternative and new traditions within all cultures, seemingly and quite often, this can ultimately start with a name and from that point, it becomes acceptable and carries with it, inspiration, love and a plethora of ideas, dreams and hope for the future.

If we now look at the Buddhist and Hindu aspects of life and the names they use, which are commonly thought of and associated with their way of life and living, we can see that once again, their names are a direct reflection and mirrored from their hearts and sense of being. Joy, Peace, Love, Compassion and Empathy are all words which we know and link with their way of life directly and without question, their teachings and philosophy, easily recognisable traits of these very sacred beings and people.

For the Buddhist people, followers of their faith and other beliefs closely connected with their way of life and teachings, everything that they are, believe in and their actions are so closely shown in all that they do and this resonates outwardly to the wider world as a whole. Once again, we can see that they take and give great pleasure in naming their young ones and babies from how they directly live, worship and respect the universe as a whole.

Throughout the wider world and all of the societies', tribes, cultures, villages, communities and many factions within all these different and extremely varied walks and paths of life, there are very individual and associated names that are bestowed upon their offspring, as we would expect there to be. This shows that as humans, we are all individuals and we have free will and choices to make, a multitude of them and our names are what we carry throughout our lives and it is these monikers, that are stamped upon us from birth, yet as we grow older, that invariably turns around, rather than the name being us, we can grow, flourish and evolve, then put our own personal stamp upon our name. These names which single us out and can, in extremes, alienate and ostracise us, can vehemently be opposed, seen as a gift that we can turn around in our favour to become a badge to be worn with singularity, strength and total pride, in who we are and what we will become.

We can all look back through the mists of time and see how much significance is upon names which we carry daily and the names that have been worn throughout history as we know it. There are infinite supplies of names that are dotted throughout the universe and will be remembered for all of eternity. Each one of us can recall names of great power, synonymous with great deeds, names which reflect total love and peace, names which have spent many years of incarceration and other names which have become infamous for whatever deeds and actions they may, or may have not done. If we reflect upon these timeless and ageless labels that have been placed upon people, we can invariably start to perceive and see the power of a name, however insignificant they may seem, names are incomprehensibly beyond power and at times, we fail to see the significance of the labels which we all wear.

Another fascinating piece that I find incredible in this jigsaw puzzle of names and lineage is that warring and opposing forces used to and still do to this day, attempt to undermine and intimidate their opponents simply in a name. Gladiators would have done this thousands of years ago as a form of scaring their opponents, Pirates named their ships in the hope of frightening anybody that ran into them at sea, marauding troops would have taken on a mantle of significant power to spread fear into the hearts of others and so on. Even today this hasn't changed and can be seen from sporting people, such as Wrestlers and Boxers using the same techniques, along with several of the warring groups around the world, all attempting to unnerve and psychically force their strength into and upon their opponents and victims. Whatever names we may carry, they are so vital and important in shaping, moulding and helping us to evolve. They can ultimately hold us back if we let them, they can infringe upon us, then again, if we flip that conception, or change our name if we choose to, they can help us to grow dramatically and then, we can wear our name badge with utter and total pride, having chosen and designated ourselves with a moniker that we are more comfortable and at ease with.

Installed within us all, whether we actually recognise it or not, is the power to create what we dream of and wish to become, along with the power, on the opposite side of the spectrum, to destroy any dreams and aspirations that we may have and wish to achieve. A name, which although can seem very mundane almost and simplistic, can bestow anything that we want it to upon us, allowing us to remain as we are and live a normal day to day life, or we can invariably hold a name which evokes infinite and unlimited possibilities upon and to the bearer and holder of that name. We only have to look at pop stars, artists, actors and a whole host of other celebrities and main stream people who have changed their names, legally, or otherwise, to basically become noticed. Many of these people felt unattached to the names they had and to help, assist and project them into the limelight further, they have chosen a more fitting and appropriate mantle for what it is they dream of and wish to be.

We can now perhaps see and comprehend just how important a name, any name can be? From what can be seen as a fleeting glimpse, thoroughly perused over, or a flash of inspiration, a name that often is seemingly plucked from out of nowhere, is the very title that we will be known as the world over, or at least the community we live in. From the first moment that we are gifted with, and then bestowed with, that very label and name will always remain with us. Even if we change it to a more preferred and appropriate name, our original stays within us always. It is this original title that has carried our ancestors and all those who stand beside us now, to this point in time and within that, we carry and hold their very essence as a part of who we are and where our roots and lineage lie. No matter what happens, we must hold all these passed and sacred beings inside our hearts, feeling and sensing them daily and in all we do. Without a single one of our ancestors, we would not and could not be who we are today. We must never overlook, nor detract from this, their lives have passed now and they are living through us, as we are them. No matter whether we like our names or not or whether we choose to adopt and become known under a different name and label, it is all these beings and loved ones that have given and gifted us our lives now, regardless of what title we have and what we wish to be known as.

The symbolism and meanings contained within a name carry great significance, if we wish them to, therefore, it is up to each one of us, as an individual, to either feel the names we have, resonate with them, or we could choose to basically ignore them and carry on regardless. It is entirely our own choice to make, neither way is wrong, or right, it is up to us to make that choice and decision.

Endowed with any title, label, moniker, or name is a great blessing and gift; firstly, it shows us that we are alive and that we exist. The pretence and importance of this shows us beyond any shadow of a doubt that we are living, breathing beings and it doesn't get any better than that. Surpassing all else, we are here to live, love, enjoy and embrace totally all the wondrous gifts that this world and universe has to offer, show and share with us All the delights contained within the world are ours to enjoy, to savour and appreciate fully and on all levels of our being and consciousness. Regardless of what we are known as, who we wish to be and what we dream and aspire to become, we must never miss the point of why we are here in the first place, which is to live life to the fullest that we can.

Whether we dislike or embrace the name we have and that we are known by, should not impede us on our life's journey, if it does, then the choice is ours to make and ours alone. We can carry it, or change it, living with, or allowing them to enhance who and what we are. This just shows and totally proves to me what is in a name. They can be and mean not a lot to us, or we can embrace the titles we have, or choose to gift ourselves with a replacement of our preference, for whatever reason and embrace either situation. No matter where in the world we live, or what we choose to do, or become, a name can mean nothing to us, or absolutely everything.

Places to hold Naming Ceremonies

A Baby naming ceremony can be as easy and free as you would like it, there are no stipulations, structures, or indoctrinations that need to be followed, or adhered to. Not to be confused with a Christening service, which is more of a religious based and very rigid process, still very enjoyable if that is your chosen path and way to name and announce the arrival of a newborn infant and child to the world.

For most of us, when a child is born into the world, we have an obligation to register their birth, usually at appointed government run and officiated buildings, the same as when we get married, or a person passes away, they all need to be officially noted down and recorded into the system. This is nothing to do with and should not be confused with a naming ceremony neither.

Venue's, place's and space's to hold a Baby naming ceremony are infinite and there is no allocated area for this. Any ceremonies performed to honour various rites, passages and landmark events are done to honour and to dedicate that moment and to show total and utter respect to your chosen Gods/ Goddesses and deities. None of these need to be structured, although there are certain ways, if you like, to bring it all together, allowing respect, honour and love to be shared freely within the ceremony, along with bringing the deities you follow and worship into being and openly sharing this with the family, loved ones and friends in attendance.

From a hilltop that is special to you, a stream, a river, or by the sea, tucked in a wooded area which holds special memories for you, a grassy area, park or even your own back garden, all of these places are perfect and it is entirely up to the individual as to their choice of place.

The significance with a naming ceremony is to announce the arrival of new life into this world, paying homage and giving respect and adoration to those who have gifted and bestowed this sacred and precious gift upon the parents, or guardians. It allows for a time of celebration, to give thanks and to follow in the footsteps of those gone before, without whom, this point in time would not and could not be possible.

When our ancestors lived in smaller villages, wooded areas and rural communities, the Mother who would have been expecting the new arrival would have often had the local wise Man, or Woman present to help assist and facilitate during the birth. It would have been an incredibly tense, nervous and anxious time for the whole community, as they waited for the imminent arrival of another member to add to their often small numbers. Upon the infant's arrival into the world, as long as everything was alright, they would have been held aloft, some of the umbilical cord still attached, along with the baby still being covered in blood, mucus and other bodily fluids. This would have been such a monumental and extremely special occasion, that often and if present, the child's Father would have held his new born Son, or Daughter, as high up in the air for all the village residents and visitors to see, pay respect to and share in this extremely special and sacred event. Acknowledging all their ancestors and their chosen Gods/Goddess', as they held aloft with immense pride the new addition to that community and the baby would have often been bestowed a name upon them at this time, literally within minutes of their arrival into the world.

Our ancestors lived very basically and without all the trappings and comforts which we now have and are accustomed to today. They lived rurally and so access to the natural world was easier and literally right outside their doors and their whole village, community, or tribe was localised within the beautiful setting of nature. They had all their ceremonies' and special events under the skies which is perfect and just how it should be, more real and nestled within all the natural surroundings which they would have been very familiar with and would have always been totally respectful to.

If we now look at the indigenous people and

communities that I reflected upon earlier, Native American Indians, the Aboriginal people of Australia and the Inuit's of the Arctic regions, they resemble and still live so closely with the natural world and very similar to how all our ancestors would have lived many, many years ago. Their daily lives and practices reflect so innately the ways of those passed and this is relevant and shows how disassociated our Western world has become in comparison to their traditions and day to day way of life and living.

Obviously, from tribe to tribe and culture to culture, ceremonies and special events do invariably change a bit, as you would expect them to, but on the whole, they are relatively similar in practice, then again, no two ceremonies are ever the same and nor should they be.

Holding aloft as a representation and paying homage, along with honouring the chosen deities, has been practiced and is a natural human response to show off new and abundant gifts, especially a new born child, has existed and been practiced since time began. It is the most obvious and widely practiced way of thanking everybody involved, physically and metaphysically that there is and like I said, it is a natural response.

From a hilltop, a mound, a sacred and recognised monument, to a river, a wooded glade, or your own back garden, all of these areas and places are perfect to give thanks and hold a ceremony in. There is nowhere that isn't appropriate, as long as you have lawful access to it; the area is entirely up to whoever is choosing the location for their special occasion. Free in the great outdoors and under the blanket of the skies and among the elements of creation, what better setting to have and hold a ceremony which is entirely based in and around the beautiful and natural world which we all inhabit and are a part of?

Quite often, the people who are choosing to have a ceremony, of any kind, usually opt for somewhere localised and sacred to them, which makes perfect sense as we connect with our surroundings and they become familiar, safe and can invariably be of great significance and extremely relevant to us. The choice is limitless and if you have a very special sacred monument you wish to hold your ceremony at, or a beautiful wooded area which holds treasured and special memories from your childhood, or somewhere similar, these are all fine and are totally acceptable. For a Baby, or child naming ceremony, things like travel, distance, noise, ease of access are all things which you may well want to think about and take into consideration, apart from those aspects, once again, you have free reign on your choice of areas and where you deem fit and sacred to you.

More and more people nowadays, especially for Baby naming ceremonies, are holding them within the safety of their own, or a family members, or friend's garden. This is ideal and a relatively easy and safe option. The place is familiar to you, access is easy, food and drinks can easily be prepared for any infants and guests there might be and it is a comfortable place which provides relative safety, which is always a good idea and always something to be considered, especially with younger ones present.

Gardens are easily decorated as well, as you can do this all in comfort and with relative ease. Altars can be placed, bunting, or flags put up, balloons can be hung and any other decorations which you would like to be placed, hung, or erected, can be done with a lot more peace of mind, rather than having to carry them all up a hill, traipsing across a field and such like, which when you have babies', infants, or any young children to worry about, can detract from what is supposed to be a very special, sacred and enjoyable occasion for all concerned. A garden is also a great venue if Babies' and infants are to be present, which invariably they will be with a Baby naming ceremony, because if the weather does decide to suddenly turn against us, rain, hail, etc, the perfect retreat of your own home is literally only a few footsteps away and all those present can be ushered in to take shelter as well. All of these ideas and unforeseen circumstances should be carefully thought about and taken into consideration, therefore allowing everybody involved to enjoy the special day, with ease, in comfort and relaxing surroundings. How each individual ceremony is performed is once again entirely up to those having it, or any officiator that may be present, who will always be relaxed enough to take those wanting the services ideas into consideration and respect their wishes and beliefs entirely.

Baby and Infant Naming Ceremonies around the World

The birth and arrival of an infant is an incredible occasion, no matter what the species is, when it happens to be the arrival of an infant child, this event is marked and celebrated by many and seen as a huge gift, a joy and a very rich blessing indeed. The very birth is recognised as a sign of new beginnings, pure and unadulterated love as well as a time of abundance, along with prosperity, hope, peace and many other positive thoughts, ideas and wishes. Hope for the future, peace for all mankind, abundance in all we strive to do and become, especially for the child whose arrival is being celebrated. New life is vehemently celebrated and so it should be. Across the world, within all cultures, all societies' and walks of life, nobody can fail to see what a very auspicious and sacred time this is. From the moment of birth, huge swathes of gratitude, joy and total thanks sweep across those who see the birth and are connected with the child. Celebrations start from the safe arrival of a child into this world and these celebrations physically manifest in a multitude of different and varying ways. As well as choosing a name before the baby is born, which is popular in a lot of the world today, there are an infinite number of ways that baby naming ceremonies happen and are performed around the world, here are a few of those ways that have been practiced for hundreds of years and are still carried on to this day within different cultures, faiths and beliefs.

In some of the Australian tribes, as with many

cultures, the naming ceremony has not changed basically since time began, traditions carry on in the same vein in which they first manifested and came into being. Within these tribes, once labour starts with the Mother to be, the Midwife, or wise woman and tribal elder is summoned to facilitate and help with the birthing process, taking care of the Mother and imminent child. The name of the child is decided by the wise woman, or elder calling out the names of the entire new arrivals family member. They start to call these names out as soon as the head appears, repeating the names until the end of the birthing process, then once the birthing sac has been expelled, the last name vocalised at that point is the chosen name, which is gifted and endowed upon the infant at that point. These tribes signify and indicate elements of nature, animals, and many other aspects of our wondrous world, so the majority of the time, the name given is more than suitable for either a male or female child.

Within the Buddhist faith, belief and way of life, they take another fascinating and interesting way of naming their newborn children. To choose a child's name, they ask an astrologer who resides within their community, to draw up a horoscope that coincides with the time of birth and other co – ordinates directly linked and associated with the child. From this horoscope, they derive and receive the initial, which will symbolise the start of the new born child's name. The naming ceremony is such a sacred occasion for them, flowers, tree leaves and other natural decorations will be scattered around, worn and given as offerings to the child and as a way of honouring the universe and all of creation, which the Buddhist's know we are all a part of and will return to upon our passing from this world.

In Chinese society a new born baby gets given two different names, with only one naming ceremony, which is another very different concept to the infinite amount of ways there are to bestow a sacred name upon a child. In Chinese culture, it is considered extremely unlucky to name a baby until they are actually born into this world. Upon birth, the new child is given a name, yet this name is only known to both parents and nobody else, which is all traditional and falls into their superstitious way of life and interpretations upon all creation. Once the child reaches, what they perceive as the landmark age of 100 days, which is the toughest part of survival in their eyes and upon surviving this period, the child is then given their adult name and a ceremony ultimately takes place at this time. Family, loved ones and friends are all invited to mark and celebrate this important milestone, where tea and food are served as the name is officially given at this celebration, welcoming the new young life into the world and the community around.

Christian's have a different procedure of naming their infants and the ceremony they have and follow is known as a Christening. The child's name is usually widely known beforehand, as with several beliefs and religions. This is the official naming day when the child will be endowed with their name/names in a Church and in the eyes of their God. Parents, family, loved ones and friends are invited to attend, usually in the local parish church where the new baby and their family reside and live. Situated within the church, will be what is known as a font, it is this, usually a large stone water vessel, which the baby will be held over, while the Vicar, or Priest, marks and anoints the child's head, with holy water from the font, with the shape of the cross, signifying and symbolising that this new born baby will follow in the tradition of Christianity and will walk in the path of God and Jesus. It is traditional for the infant on this very sacred day, to wear what is known as a Christening gown. These are white and show purification and these gowns can be and often are handed down from generation to generation, indicating belief, lineage and new life.

The Inuit people, who inhabit and reside in the arctic regions of the Northern hemisphere, have another way of choosing their baby's names. During pregnancy, if a family member, or loved one, passes away during this nine month period, it is often the deceased person's name that will inevitable be gifted and endowed upon the infant. It is their belief, as it is with many people around the world, that life, even if passed, it continues and goes on, just in another form. It is by gifting a deceased ones name upon a new life, which shows this and is a beautiful way of remembering that person. This same practice has been in effect since time began and can be seen within many walks of life, different cultures and faiths around the world, even to this day. A beautiful and very special way of signifying and remembering those gone, celebrating with the new life and energy of a child. If a loved one doesn't die during the pregnancy term, which hopefully they don't, then another way of naming comes into being. Once the baby is born, there is usually some identifiable birth mark, a spot, or some sort of individual marking. A name is taken or connected with this marking and a name is linked and taken from this.

The Jewish faith has another different take on the way they name their infants and it is different for a boy and a girl. Once the baby is born, if it is a little girl, their naming ceremony can be performed at any time while they are at their Synagogue having readings from their holy book, known as the Torah. For a baby boy, their naming normally takes place when they are eight days old; this coincides with their belief and practice of all boys being surgically circumcised at that time and age of their young lives. After the naming ceremony has been performed, family and friends toast the baby, enjoy food and drink together and gifts are given for the baby. Blessings and prayers are vocalised by guests to bring health, abundance and prosperity for and to the newly named child.

There are several different takes and practices of baby naming throughout the Native American Indian tribes of the USA. One that I find really beautiful is practiced and is traditional for the Hopi tribe of Arizona, is as follows. When the newly born infant is twenty days old, family and guests gather to say prayers and offer gifts for the child. They share food made with corn, which is the symbol of life for the Hopi. Offerings of corn are left outside as a symbol of thanks and gratitude, also to honour the earth; basically to give thanks for all that they have in their lives, along with the new life that has just been born. Then, just before sunrise, the child's Grand Mother carries the infant outside, holds the child aloft in the direction of the Sun and then announces and bestows the name upon the child.

Paganism is probably the oldest faith, belief, or tradition known in and around the world. Many alternate beliefs and religions use age old Pagan beliefs and ways, basically adopting them and incorporating them into their own structured belief system. Many ceremonies performed in other paths and beliefs, originate and can be directly linked to the age old ways of Paganism. As old as time itself, the Pagan ways have encompassed the entire natural world and take their way of life and beliefs from nature itself. A Pagan baby naming ceremony is another beautiful, non evasive and totally natural occasion, practiced since time began and now lends itself to the services performed by many others around and across the globe. Held within a wooded glade, or area, by a stream, a river, on a hill, anywhere really that is accessible and outside within nature. The guests form a circle around the celebrant, or officiate, who stands with the parents, or guardian. Honour is paid to the elements and chosen deities, guests are invited to say a few words, sing, recite poetry, etc and during this, the infant is held aloft while thanks is given to the Sun, Moon and everything contained within this beautiful world. The child's name is called out and witness is given by all the guests, along with the elements and spirits around. The young child is often then passed around so that the guests can hold them and be officially introduced to this new and beautiful arrival who has recently arrived and been born to this world. This Pagan ceremony is not too structured and can be performed from any age. Once again, this ceremony will normally include food and drink being consumed by all the guests, along with total thanks to the natural world and all who live and reside within it.

Within some African tribes and communities, they take a different stance on the naming of a newborn infant; they let the child choose their own name, at random, but still a very beautiful way of doing things. Family members and friends all choose a name, earth and nature based. They then write the word, or a drawing to symbolise it. The individual pieces of paper, dried fruit skins, or animal hides, are then folded up and placed together in a small basket, or bowl. Someone, normally one of the child's parents, holds the infant while their hand enters the container. Whichever piece of skin, paper, etc is grabbed by the baby first, becomes that child's name and a naming ceremony ensues straight afterwards, with dancing, along with food and drink being offered to all present.

Conclusion

This book has, as with writing any book or article, been an incredible adventure and a wonderful journey to go on. I sincerely hope that you have enjoyed it as much as I have enjoyed the writing and compiling it. When we actually take a look and reflect upon what a name is, how they came into being and the wider use and symbolism of them, we are opening up what is really an infinite subject and topic. Once we take all of that into account and consideration we can then appreciate the meanings and how many names have come into existence and have been used for hundreds of years and across the world, within many cultures and societies around the globe.

The significance of naming a child supersedes many tangible ideas and aspirations we may hold for them as individuals. To be given the gift and blessing of naming a child is indeed an honour. Not only are you bestowing a label upon them to shout when they do something wrong, you are gifting one of the most important titles, labels and the name which they will be held accountable for and be recognised from, not just throughout their lives, but for the rest of time to come. For any of you nowadays that may have used a computer to search for your ancestors, you will realise what I am saying. Each name is recorded now, not only in the mists of time for all of eternity, but also within the technological modern world we are each a part of and inhabit daily.

Thank you to you all for reading my words and once again, I hope they have made you think, maybe answered some questions you had, or at least provided an alternative point of view?

Blessings and much love to each and every one of you.

John Awen   / | \

Lightning Source UK Ltd.
Milton Keynes UK
UKHW020826060223
416538UK00016B/1922

9 780995 547803